Table of C

Table of Content..1
Chapter 1: Introduction 2
Chapter 2: William the Conqueror 7
Chapter 3: Henry VIII and the Tudors 13
Chapter 4: The Stuarts and the English Civil War 16
Chapter 5: The Glorious Revolution and the Hanoverians 22
Chapter 6: Victoria and the British Empire 27
Chapter 7: The Windsors and the World Wars.......................33
Chapter 8: Elizabeth II and modern monarchy 39
Chapter 9: The future of the British monarchy......................44
Chapter 10: Conclusion 50

Chapter 1: Introduction

Brief overview of the British monarchy

From its early origins in the medieval period, the British monarchy has played a pivotal role in shaping the nation's history and identity. The Norman Conquest of 1066 marked a turning point, as William the Conqueror introduced a centralized monarchy to England. Since then, the monarchy has continued to evolve, with significant figures such as King Henry VIII and Queen Elizabeth I leaving indelible marks on the institution.

The constitutional role of the British monarchy has undergone significant changes over time. While once holding absolute power, the monarchy gradually transitioned into a constitutional monarchy, with limited powers and a focus on ceremonial duties. Today, the British monarch serves as the head of state, representing the unity of the nation, but holds limited political powers. The sovereign's role is primarily symbolic, as the practical exercise of governance rests with elected officials and the parliament.

One of the most distinctive features of the British monarchy is its rich ceremonial and ritualistic traditions that have been preserved through the ages. These ceremonies serve to reinforce the continuity of the monarchy and embody the pomp and grandeur associated with it. Events such as the State Opening of Parliament, the Changing of the Guard at Buckingham Palace, and the Coronation ceremony itself demonstrate the heritage and pageantry that define the monarchy.

In addition to ceremonial duties, the British monarchy also performs various official and diplomatic roles. The Queen acts as a symbol of national unity and carries out numerous state visits, both within the United Kingdom and abroad. Additionally, the sovereign undertakes the vital task of granting royal assent to legislation, endorsing the will of the elected parliament. Although this process is largely ceremonial, it signifies the collaboration between the monarchy and the parliamentary system, anchoring the institution within the broader democratic framework.

Despite its traditional nature, the British monarchy has managed to adapt and remain relevant in contemporary British society. The royal family consistently engages with the public, participating in charitable causes and fulfilling public engagements. This accessibility and the monarchy's philanthropic efforts have endeared the royal family to the public, making them a cherished and respected institution. Additionally, the younger generation of royals, such as the Duke and Duchess of Cambridge and the Duke and Duchess of Sussex, have brought renewed energy and a modern touch to the monarchy, further enhancing its appeal.

Moreover, the British monarchy continues to have a unifying role within the United Kingdom. Its presence transcends political divisions, providing a sense of stability and continuity. This is particularly evident during times of national celebration and crisis, where the monarch's presence and measured response can foster a sense of solidarity and resilience among the British people. Furthermore, the monarchy has successfully embraced the power of symbolism, reflecting and representing the rich cultural diversity of the United Kingdom. From its origins as an absolutist power, it has evolved into a constitutional monarchy, with limited powers and a focus on ceremonial duties. Its rich traditions and ceremonial obligations contribute to its enduring appeal, while its ability to adapt has ensured its place within contemporary British society. The British monarchy's unique role, combining constitutional and ceremonial functions, as well as its continuous engagement with the public, exemplifies its significance in both historical and contemporary contexts.

Importance of monarchs in British history

One of the most crucial contributions of monarchs in British history is their ability to serve as unifying forces. Throughout the centuries, Britain has experienced internal conflicts, regional rivalries, and political divisions. Monarchs, with their hereditary authority and central position, have often played the vital role of unifying the nation under a common identity. From the reign of King Alfred the Great, who defended the kingdom against Viking invasions and laid the foundations of the English monarchy, to Queen Elizabeth II, whose symbolic role as the head of state unites people from different regions and backgrounds, monarchs have acted as the binding force that holds Britain together.

Moreover, monarchs have served as advocates of stability in times of political turbulence. In periods of uncertainty and unrest, such as the Wars of the Roses or the English Civil War, the continuity and legitimacy provided by a stable monarchy proved indispensable. The monarch's position as a figurehead, endowed with a sense of divine right, has been a crucial stabilizing force in the face of political upheavals. Their presence has provided reassurance to the people, ensuring a sense of continuity and order even amidst chaos.

In addition to their political roles, monarchs have also held immense cultural significance throughout British history. They have served as patrons of the arts, fostering an environment conducive to artistic expression and intellectual development. Countless monarchs, such as King Henry VIII, Queen Elizabeth I, and King George III, were known for their passion for literature, music, and the visual arts. Their patronage not only laid the groundwork for the flourishing of art, literature, and science but also helped shape the cultural identity of Britain. The grand architectural marvels, the iconic portraits, and the incomparable literary works of British history owe a great debt to the support and encouragement provided by monarchs.

Furthermore, monarchs have been instrumental in promoting advancements in science, exploration, and industry. The Age of Enlightenment, marked by significant scientific breakthroughs and intellectual progress, saw several British monarchs actively supporting these endeavors. King Charles II played a pivotal role in establishing the Royal Society, which promoted scientific research and helped lay the foundations of modern science. Similarly, Queen Victoria's reign witnessed the Industrial Revolution, transforming Britain into a global leader in technology and trade. The monarch's role in fostering an environment conducive to innovation and progress cannot be overstated, as these advancements have left an indelible mark on the nation's history and global influence.

It is essential to note that the influence of monarchs in British history extends beyond political and cultural realms. They have also played a crucial role in shaping the legal framework and governance of the nation. Magna Carta, a document that laid the groundwork for many principles of modern democracy, was signed by King John in 1215. This historical event marked a significant step towards limiting the absolute power of the monarchy and instituting important legal rights and protections for the people. Similarly, subsequent monarchs, such as King William III and Queen Mary II, played instrumental roles in the evolution of the constitutional monarchy, leading to the gradual shift of power from the monarchy to elected representatives. They have acted as unifying figures, advocates of stability, and cultural icons throughout the centuries. Monarchs have played pivotal roles in shaping politics, promoting culture, fostering scientific advancements, and influencing the legal frameworks of the nation. Their enduring presence and influence have left an indelible mark on the identity, development, and trajectory of Britain. Whether through the centralized power they represent, their patronage of the arts and sciences, or their contributions to the governance of the nation, monarchs have cemented their place as integral figures in the tapestry of British history.

Chapter 2: William the Conqueror

The Norman Conquest of England in 1066

Known as the Norman Conquest, this extraordinary event saw the powerful Norman invaders successfully claim the English throne, reshaping the course of the nation for centuries to come. In this one, we will delve into the key aspects of the Norman Conquest, analyzing the events leading up to it, examining the names and faces behind this transformative conquest, and exploring its lasting impact on England's society, politics, and legal system.

I. Background:
In order to truly comprehend the significance of the Norman Conquest, it is vital to explore its historical context. Prior to 1066, England had been a predominantly Anglo-Saxon kingdom, with deep-rooted Anglo-Saxon institutions and cultural norms. However, after the death of Edward the Confessor, the English throne found itself amidst a disputed succession. This power vacuum acted as a catalyst for multiple claimants to the throne, leading to the eventual invasion by Norman forces under the leadership of William, Duke of Normandy.

II. The Actors of the Conquest:
At the forefront of the Norman Conquest stood William, known by history as William the Conqueror, whose ambition and strategic acumen paved the way for his success. William

maneuvered skillfully, defeating Harold II, the last Anglo-Saxon king, in the iconic Battle of Hastings. But William's triumph was not solely his own achievement; it relied on the cooperation and shared ambitions of his loyal barons and allies. Understanding the personalities and roles of influential figures such as Odo of Bayeux, William FitzOsbern, and William de Warenne is crucial to grasping the intricacies of the Norman Conquest.

III. Battle of Hastings and the Aftermath:
The clash at Hastings in 1066 shaped the destiny of England. The battle itself was a turning point, highlighting the military prowess of the Normans and the ultimate defeat of the Anglo-Saxon forces. The triumphant William ascended to the throne, establishing Norman rule over England. Through a comprehensive understanding of the battle and its aftermath, one can gain insight into the series of events that led to the consolidation of Norman power and authority, reshaping Britain's political landscape.

IV. The Normans in England:
The Norman Conquest brought with it an influx of Norman elites and their distinct cultural practices. These newcomers, now occupying the highest echelons of English society, had a profound impact on the existing structures of power and social norms. We will explore how language, architecture, legal systems, and the very fabric of everyday life in England underwent radical transformations under Norman influence. The mutual influence between the Normans and Anglo-Saxons also led to the gradual fusion of the two cultures, creating a unique blend that would define the identity of England for centuries to come.

V. Legal and Political Transformations:

One of the most enduring legacies of the Norman Conquest lies in the transformation it brought about in England's legal and political systems. The introduction of Norman feudalism, intricate systems of governance, and the establishment of an efficient administrative apparatus, known as the Exchequer, laid the foundation for a centralized and highly organized state. We will explore how these legal and political changes influenced the evolution of England's legal system and provided the groundwork for future political developments, including the Magna Carta in the thirteenth century.

The Norman Conquest of England in 1066 undoubtedly stands as a seminal event in British history. Its impact was profound, forever altering the political, cultural, and societal fabric of England. By understanding the historical context, key players, battles, and subsequent impact of this conquest, we can appreciate the magnitude of its consequences. The Norman Conquest continues to shape the identity of England, leaving an indelible mark on subsequent generations and reminding us of the interconnectedness of history and the transformative power of conquest.

William's impact on English society and culture

His conquest of England in 1066 completely transformed the country, ushering in a new era with lasting effects on English society and culture. This essay aims to explore the multifaceted impact of William on the various aspects of English life, ranging from governance and language to architecture and social hierarchy. By delving into these areas, we will gain a deeper appreciation of the significant role William played in shaping the trajectory of English society and culture.

Governance and Legal Systems:
One of the most significant changes brought about by William's conquest was the establishment of a centralized governance system. He introduced a strong monarchy that replaced the decentralization prevalent during Anglo-Saxon times. William's consolidation of power allowed for a more efficient administration, resulting in improved law enforcement, taxation, and judicial systems. The Domesday Book, a detailed survey conducted during William's reign, helped standardize land ownership and provide a comprehensive record of English properties. These developments laid the foundation for a more organized, accountable, and unified governance system that shaped English society for centuries to come.

Language and Literature:
An enduring legacy of William lies in his contribution to the development of the English language. Prior to the Norman Conquest, English (Old English) was the dominant language spoken by the populace. However, after William's ascension to the throne, Norman French became the language of the ruling elite, while English primarily remained a language spoken by the commoners. This linguistic divide led to the emergence of Middle English, a fusion of Old English and Norman French, which eventually became the language of Chaucer and other famed medieval poets. William's impact on language serves as a testament to the cultural exchanges and linguistic assimilation that shaped English identity in subsequent centuries.

Architecture and the Built Environment:
The Norman Conquest brought about a distinctive architectural and cultural shift, evident in the remarkable Norman style of building that quickly gained popularity. The Normans introduced towering castles and magnificent cathedrals across England, replacing the simpler Anglo-Saxon structures. These architectural marvels not only showcased Norman power but also influenced English society by defining the landscape and reinforcing the social order. The castles, serving as symbols of authority and military dominance, played a crucial role in establishing control and consolidating power. Additionally, the introduction of monastic orders like the Cistercians during William's reign greatly influenced ecclesiastical architecture and monastic life, leaving an indelible mark on English culture and spirituality.

Social Hierarchy and Feudalism:
William's conquest fundamentally changed the social fabric of England, introducing a feudal system that would shape English society for centuries. He rewarded his loyal followers with vast tracts of land, establishing a hierarchical structure where landowners, or lords, held power over their vassals through complex feudal obligations. This system created a stratified society, with the king at the top and the peasantry at the bottom. The profound effects of feudalism on English social structure and the relationship between lord and peasant endured well beyond William's reign, leaving an enduring impact on English society and its class divisions.

William the Conqueror's impact on English society and culture cannot be overstated. His conquest and subsequent reign laid the foundation for an organized governance system, endowed the English language with a rich linguistic tapestry, introduced iconic architecture, and established a hierarchal social structure through feudalism. The multifaceted legacy of William's influence continues to shape modern England, acting as a constant reminder of the transformative power of historical events and the indelible mark left on cultures and societies. By understanding the depths of William's impact, we gain invaluable insight into the foundations and evolution of English society and culture.

Chapter 3: Henry VIII and the Tudors

Henry VIII's break from the Catholic Church

To fully grasp the reasons behind Henry VIII's break from the Catholic Church, it is essential to consider the political climate of the time. The early sixteenth century witnessed the rise of Protestant movements across Europe, challenging the religious and political authority of the Catholic Church. These movements, coupled with the influence of humanist ideas, created an atmosphere of change and reform. Henry, a young and ambitious monarch, was not immune to these shifting tides. His reign was characterized by a desire for control, both politically and personally. Breaking away from the Catholic Church allowed Henry to consolidate power, as he could now claim ultimate authority over religious matters within his realm.

Religion played a significant role in the decision to break from the Catholic Church. At the heart of the matter was Henry's desire to divorce his first wife, Catherine of Aragon, due to her inability to produce a male heir. However, this request was met with resistance from the Pope, who was heavily influenced by the political environment and the power dynamics of Europe. Frustrated by the Pope's refusal to grant an annulment, Henry sought a solution that would allow him to secure a divorce and establish his own religious authority. This led to the creation of the Church of England, with Henry as its Supreme Head. By divorcing Catherine and marrying Anne Boleyn, Henry could not only secure a potential male heir but also solidify his newfound power as the head of an independent church.

While personal motivations certainly played a role, Henry VIII's break from the Catholic Church cannot be fully understood without considering the wider consequences and impact. The repercussions of this decision were profound, reverberating throughout the religious, social, and political fabric of England. The Church of England, also known as the Anglican Church, became the established church of the realm, bringing significant changes in doctrine and practice. Monastic institutions were dissolved, wealth was redistributed, and the English Reformation took hold. For the first time in centuries, England found itself at odds with the Papacy, marking a fundamental shift in its religious allegiance.

The break from the Catholic Church also had significant political implications, both domestically and internationally. Henry's rejection of the Pope's authority opened the door for greater centralized control, as the king now wielded both religious and political power. This newfound authority enabled Henry to suppress dissent and silence opposition, effectively solidifying his position as an absolute monarch. However, these actions also led to religious divisions and conflicts within England, as those who remained loyal to the Catholic Church faced persecution and discrimination.

Internationally, Henry's break from Rome had repercussions beyond England's borders. The Catholic Church, already weakened by the Protestant Reformation, saw the loss of one of its most powerful and influential kingdoms. This shift of allegiance had diplomatic and strategic consequences, as England sought new alliances and forged closer ties with Protestant states, in particular, Germany and Scandinavia. This aligning with the Protestant cause had long-lasting effects on the geopolitical landscape of Europe, shaping the course of religious and political relations for years to come. Driven by political ambition, personal desires, and a changing religious landscape, Henry's decision to break with the Catholic Church set in motion a series of events that forever altered the course of English history. The establishment of the Church of England, the dissolution of monasteries, and the subsequent religious and political divisions marked a revolutionary period of change and reform. Understanding the motivations, context, and impact of this momentous decision is imperative to fully grasp the nuanced complexities of this extraordinary event.

Chapter 4: The Stuarts and the English Civil War

Charles I's reign and execution

From his controversial policies to his eventual execution, Charles I's reign was marked by a power struggle between the monarchy and Parliament which ultimately led to a revolution and the establishment of a republic. In this comprehensive analysis, we will delve into the key events, policies, and influences that shaped Charles I's reign, and examine the circumstances surrounding his execution.

1. The Early Years of Charles I's Reign:

Charles I ascended to the throne in 1625, following the death of his father, James I. His reign was marked by numerous challenges, including conflicts with Parliament and religious tensions between Protestants and Catholics. Charles's personal beliefs and his penchant for favoring Catholic advisors created a divide among the political elite and heightened public unease. These tensions set the stage for the turbulent years that would define his reign.

2. The Divine Right of Kings and Royal Authority:

Central to Charles I's reign was his firm belief in the "divine right of kings," a doctrine that proclaimed the monarch as God's representative on earth and granted them absolute power. This ideology clashed with the growing power and influence of Parliament, leading to protracted clashes between Charles and the House of Commons. This struggle for supremacy between the monarchy and Parliament laid the foundation for future political upheaval.

3. The Petition of Right and its Implications:

In 1628, Charles I was forced to concede to the demands of Parliament by signing the Petition of Right. This significant document sought to limit the king's power by affirming certain constitutional rights, such as habeas corpus, and challenging arbitrary taxation and imprisonment. Despite initially accepting the Petition, Charles later dismissed Parliament, sparking further discontent and sowing the seeds of revolution.

4. The Personal Rule and Charles's Religious Policies:

Following the dissolution of Parliament, Charles I pursued a period of personal rule, during which he governed without parliamentary interference for over a decade. This period saw the introduction of policies that further ignited religious tensions. Charles's attempts to impose a uniform liturgy throughout his kingdoms, particularly in Scotland, resulted in widespread resistance and ultimately triggered armed conflicts such as the Bishops' Wars.

5. The Outbreak of the English Civil War:

The 1640s witnessed the escalation of conflicts between Charles

I and Parliament, leading to the outbreak of the English Civil War. This protracted and brutal war was primarily fought between the royalist supporters of Charles and the forces of Parliament led by Oliver Cromwell. The war highlighted fundamental differences in political ideologies, with Parliamentarians advocating for a constitutional monarchy, while Charles remained steadfast in his belief in absolute royal authority.

6. The Trial and Execution of Charles I:

With the defeat of royalist forces in 1646, Charles I was eventually taken into custody by Parliament. In 1649, he was put on trial for high treason, a momentous event that shook the foundations of the monarchy. The trial, led by Oliver Cromwell and other prominent figures, resulted in Charles I's condemnation and execution by beheading. This event marked the first time in English history that a reigning monarch had been held accountable in such a manner.

The reign and execution of Charles I revealed the complexity of power dynamics in seventeenth-century England. The struggles between the monarchy and Parliament, conflicts arising from religious tensions, and the ultimate execution of Charles I impacted the country for years to come. The repercussions of this era continue to shape discussions on constitutional monarchy, religious freedom, and the balance of power to this day. By examining this tumultuous period, we gain valuable insights into the evolving nature of governance and the social forces that shape nations.

Oliver Cromwell and the Commonwealth

The English Commonwealth, or the Commonwealth of England, Scotland, and Ireland, was established in 1649 following the execution of King Charles I. This marked a radical departure from the traditional monarchical system, as power was vested in a Council of State and later in a single ruler known as the Lord Protector. Cromwell became the dominant political figure within the Commonwealth, leading military campaigns and exerting his authority over the nation.

Cromwell's journey towards prominence began with his military successes during the English Civil War. As a key leader of the Parliamentarian forces, he proved himself to be an astute general, winning significant battles against the Royalists. His renowned victory at the Battle of Naseby in 1645 decisively shifted the tides in favor of Parliament, leading to the subsequent end of the war.

These military triumphs propelled Cromwell into a position of influence within the Commonwealth. In 1653, he dissolved Parliament and assumed the role of Lord Protector, effectively making him the de facto ruler of England. Cromwell held this position until his death in 1658, leaving behind a complex legacy that continues to provoke scholarly debate.

At the heart of Cromwell's rule was his fervent Puritan faith, which shaped both his personal convictions and his vision for the nation. Puritanism, a religious movement emphasizing piety, moral discipline, and a desire for social reform, held significant sway during this period. Cromwell saw himself as a devout servant of God, viewing his actions as part of a divine mission to purify and unite the nation.

The Commonwealth under Cromwell witnessed profound changes in various aspects of society. One of the most striking examples was the abolition of the monarchy, a bold step that reflected the republicanism prevailing within the Commonwealth. Yet despite distaste for monarchy, Cromwell initially declined the offer to become king, refusing to undermine the principles of the Republic. Instead, he adopted the title of Lord Protector, blending monarchical symbolism with republican governance.

Cromwell's rule also had a profound impact on foreign relations. The Commonwealth faced external threats from European powers, while Cromwell himself sought to spread his Puritan ideals beyond England's borders. His military campaigns extended English influence across Europe, most notably his defeat of the Dutch Republic and his involvement in the Anglo-Spanish war. Cromwell's expansionist goals were tied to his belief in a providential mission to promote religious liberty and challenge Catholicism.

The relationship between Cromwell's government and the people of the Commonwealth was complex. While he championed religious freedom and embraced a degree of toleration, dissenting religious groups were frequently persecuted, particularly those deemed radical or disruptive to the established order. Cromwell's regime was marked by a delicate balancing act, attempting to maintain stability while confronting dissent and upholding his vision of a godly nation.

With Cromwell's death in 1658, the Commonwealth faced an uncertain future. Cromwell's successors lacked his charisma and political acumen, leading to internal divisions and a gradual decline in the viability of the Republican experiment. In 1660, the monarchy was restored, and the Commonwealth officially came to an end.

Today, the legacy of Oliver Cromwell and the Commonwealth is complex and contentious. For some, Cromwell is seen as a champion of liberty and justice, a figure who challenged the establishment and fostered radical change. Others view him as a tyrant, responsible for religious persecution and authoritarian rule. The intricacies of the Commonwealth and Cromwell's role within it require careful examination and critical analysis to fully understand a period that shaped the trajectory of British history. As a military leader, political figure, and religious zealot, he transformed the nation during a time of tumultuous change. The Commonwealth represented a bold experiment in republican governance, driven by Cromwell's vision of a godly nation. Although the Commonwealth ultimately collapsed, its influence on subsequent political and social developments is undeniable. By exploring the complexities of Cromwell's rule and the ideologies that guided him, we can gain a deeper understanding of this transformative period in English history.

Chapter 5: The Glorious Revolution and the Hanoverians

William III and Mary II's joint rule

The joint rule of William of Orange and Mary II began in 1688 with the Glorious Revolution, a bloodless coup d'état that left an indelible mark on British history. The revolution had its roots in tensions between the Protestant majority and the Catholic minority in England. Concerns over the succession of James II, a staunch Catholic, led to a coalition inviting William, a Protestant and Dutch Stadtholder, to claim the throne alongside his wife, James II's Protestant daughter, Mary. This joint reign, founded on principles of religious tolerance and respect for the rule of law, sought to heal the divisions within the realm.

One of the immediate challenges faced by William and Mary was solidifying their claim to the throne, as the legitimacy of their rule was questioned by some loyalists to James II. This complex and sensitive issue was navigated with skill and diplomacy. To strengthen their position, William and Mary agreed to the Declaration of Rights in 1689, which outlined the rights and liberties of the people and curtailed the powers of the monarchy. This document, along with the Bill of Rights that followed, enshrined principles like parliamentary sovereignty, free elections, and the right to petition the monarch, laying down the foundations for a constitutional monarchy.

William and Mary's reign also saw significant military and political challenges. The threat of the exiled James II, along with his Catholic allies in Europe, loomed large. William's military prowess and astute diplomacy allowed him to rally Protestant forces and secure the realm against external threats. The victory at the Battle of the Boyne in 1690, where William decisively defeated James II, cemented his position as a respected and capable leader. Additionally, the signing of the Treaty of Ryswick in 1697 marked the end of the Nine Years' War and brought relative stability to Britain.

It is crucial to note that the joint rule of William and Mary brought about fundamental shifts in the balance of power, particularly between the monarchy and Parliament. The monarchs' willingness to share power and cooperate with Parliament set a precedent for future rulers. Their approach to governance emphasized accountability, consultation, and compromises between the crown and elected representatives. This era witnessed the beginning of the establishment of cabinet government, with William appointing trusted advisors, who would later form the basis of the modern-day Cabinet.

In addition to political and military achievements, William and Mary's reign introduced a cultural and intellectual flowering, commonly referred to as the "Glorious Revolution culture." This cultural movement saw a surge in artistic endeavors, scientific exploration, and the rise of political thinkers, such as John Locke, whose ideas on natural rights and limited government influenced the shaping of the British political landscape. The freedom of thought and expression nurtured during this time had a profound impact on the Enlightenment era that followed, setting the stage for scientific and intellectual advancements.

Moreover, William and Mary's joint rule also brought significant changes within the realms of religion and religious tolerance. While England had been historically divided along religious lines, the Glorious Revolution marked a turning point in creating a more inclusive and tolerant society. This was exemplified by the Act of Toleration of 1689, granting limited rights of worship to Protestant dissenters and protecting them from persecution. However, it is important to acknowledge that Catholics were still subjected to various restrictions and discriminations during this period. Their reign laid the groundwork for a constitutional monarchy based on shared power, rule of law, and respect for individual rights and liberties. This era witnessed pivotal political, military, and cultural developments that set the stage for the subsequent years of British history. The legacy of William and Mary's reign can still be felt today, serving as a powerful reminder of the importance and benefits of cooperation, compromise, and a government based on principles of accountability and popular consent.

Hanoverian succession and George III

This period marked a transition in political power, as the Hanoverian dynasty came to the throne after the death of Queen Anne in 1714. George I, followed by his son George II, laid the foundation for the eventual ascension of George III to the British throne. This essay aims to explore the Hanoverian succession, its implications for British society, and delve into the fascinating reign of King George III, known for both his achievements and the challenges he faced during his tenure as monarch.

The Hanoverian Succession:
The Hanoverian succession refers to the transfer of power from the Stuart dynasty to the Hanoverian dynasty in 1714. This transition was driven by the absence of any direct Protestant heirs to the British throne within the Stuart family. The Act of Settlement 1701, which aimed to ensure the stability of the monarchy by securing a Protestant succession, played a pivotal role in paving the way for the Hanoverian dynasty. It named Sophia of Hanover, a Protestant descendant of James VI and I, as the next in line for the throne. However, Sophia passed away before Queen Anne, leading to her son, George I, ascending to the throne upon Anne's death.

Implications for British Society:
The Hanoverian succession brought about significant changes to British society. The new dynasty stemmed from the German House of Hanover, leading to a blending of German and British influences in the country's political structure. This infusion of continental ideas played a crucial role in shaping British politics, diplomacy, and even cultural exchanges in the ensuing years. Moreover, George I and George II brought with them a newfound stability and focus on parliamentary government, establishing the monarchy as a constitutional figurehead. This shift towards a constitutional monarchy encouraged greater involvement of the people in political affairs, ultimately laying the groundwork for democratic institutions that define the British system today.

Reign of George III:
The reign of King George III, which spanned from 1760 to 1820, was both remarkable and tumultuous. Known widely as the

"Mad King," George III faced a series of challenges that tested his abilities as a monarch and his mental stability. His reign witnessed both the American Revolutionary War and the Napoleonic Wars, which tested the limits of the British Empire. However, it would be unfair to solely focus on the hardships faced by George III without acknowledging his positive contributions.

George III played a pivotal role in stabilizing the monarchy and strengthening the institution of constitutional monarchy. He was known for his firm belief in his duty to his people, which he exhibited through his devotion to public duties, philanthropy, and patronage of the arts. Additionally, George III's support for the industrial revolution and agricultural innovations helped shape Britain into an economic powerhouse. His reign also witnessed major advancements in science, exploration, and literature, with figures such as James Cook and Jane Austen emerging as significant figures of the time.

The Hanoverian succession marked a crucial turning point in British history, with the ascension of the Hanoverian dynasty and subsequent reign of King George III. These events brought about profound changes in British society and politics, paving the way for the development of democratic institutions and a constitutional monarchy. While George III's reign faced numerous challenges, his contributions to the stability of the monarchy and support for advancements in various fields cannot be overlooked. This period played a critical role in shaping modern Britain and remains a defining one in its rich history.

Chapter 6: Victoria and the British Empire

Queen Victoria's long reign

When Queen Victoria ascended the throne at the young age of 18, Britain was experiencing a transformative period known as the Victorian era. Industrialization was in full swing, bringing unprecedented advancements in manufacturing, transportation, and communication. The young queen quickly adapted to these changes and became a symbol of stability and continuity during a time of rapid progress. While many monarchs of the era held limited power, Victoria's reign stood out as one in which the monarchy played a significant role in shaping the nation's policies and institutions.

One of the hallmarks of Queen Victoria's reign was the expansion of the British Empire. Great Britain became the world's preeminent colonial power, with territories spanning continents and oceans. Victoria's rule witnessed the incorporation of vast territories, including India, Canada, Australia, and parts of Africa, into the British Empire. This expansion brought with it enormous responsibilities and challenges, as well as controversy surrounding the repercussions of colonialism. Through her leadership and steadfast commitment to her role, Queen Victoria instilled a sense of imperial pride in her subjects and fostered a national identity rooted in the idea of a global empire.

Despite her early reputation as the "Widow of Windsor" following the death of her beloved husband, Prince Albert, Queen Victoria's reign was marked by a deep emotional connection with her people. She became a symbol of emotional stability and resilience, transcending the boundaries of class and societal norms. Her genuine concern for the well-being of her subjects, especially during times of hardship such as the Irish potato famine and the Crimean War, endeared her to the hearts of the British people. Victoria's attention to the needs and concerns of her subjects helped bolster the monarchy's popularity and reaffirmed the institution's relevance in an increasingly democratic society.

Queen Victoria was not limited to mere symbolic gestures; she actively engaged in political affairs. With a keen interest in state affairs, she developed strong relationships with her Prime Ministers and exerted influence in shaping government policies. Her letters and diaries, meticulously recorded over her long reign, provide fascinating insights into her thoughts and opinions on a wide range of issues, including political matters and social reforms. Queen Victoria's active involvement in politics, albeit within the constitutional boundaries of her role, showcased her determination to use her influence for the betterment of the nation.

Throughout her reign, Queen Victoria maintained a strong commitment to cultural and artistic endeavors, elevating the status of the monarchy as a patron of the arts. This period witnessed a proliferation of literature, poetry, and visual arts, often referred to as the Victorian cultural renaissance. Notable figures such as Charles Dickens, Lord Alfred Tennyson, and the Pre-Raphaelite Brotherhood emerged during this time, producing works that both reflected and influenced the social and political changes happening in Britain. By recognizing and encouraging the contributions of artists, Queen Victoria helped shape the cultural identity of her era and fostered a climate of creativity and expression.

It is impossible to discuss Queen Victoria's reign without acknowledging the significant changes that occurred in British society during this time. The Victorian era is often associated with strict morals and social conventions, but it also witnessed the birth of social movements and reforms that aimed to address the widening social inequalities of the industrialized nation. The push for women's rights, the abolition of slavery, and the labor movement all gained momentum during Queen Victoria's reign. Though she held conservative views on certain matters, Victoria's reign saw advancements towards a more inclusive and egalitarian society. Her reign witnessed the great rise of the British Empire, transformative social and political changes, and a remarkable cultural renaissance. By embodying stability, emotional connection, and political engagement, Queen Victoria left an enduring legacy as a powerful and influential monarch. Her reign continues to captivate the imagination of historians, scholars, and the general public, inviting us to delve deeper into the complexities and triumphs of a remarkable era.

Expansion of the British Empire

As we delve into the topic of the British Empire's expansion, it is crucial to remember that this vast empire was not built overnight. Its roots can be traced back to the late 16th century with the establishment of English colonies in the Americas, such as Jamestown in Virginia. However, it was during the 18th and 19th centuries that the empire truly began to flourish, as Britain's naval dominance and industrial revolution provided the perfect environment for expansive endeavors.

One of the key driving forces behind the expansion of the British Empire was economic motives. The empire became a hub for trade, with colonies acting as sources of raw materials, such as cotton, sugar, and tea, which were essential for Britain's developing industries. Moreover, these colonies provided vast markets for British manufactured goods, reinforcing the economic interdependence between the metropole and its colonies. The lust for economic prosperity propelled British explorers, merchants, and settlers to venture into uncharted territories, navigating treacherous seas and negotiating with indigenous populations.

Central to the expansion of the British Empire was also the aspect of power projection. The empire not only sought to gain economic benefits but also to project its military and political strength across the globe. By establishing strong naval bases and fortifications, Britain ensured its dominance over trade routes and maintained a strategic advantage over other imperial powers. This led to the acquisition of territories like Gibraltar, Malta, and Singapore, securing British control over critical chokepoints in the world's oceans. These military installations often served as symbols of British power, reminding both allies and rivals of the empire's might.

Cultural and ideological factors must also be considered when examining the expansion of the British Empire. The British, driven by a sense of superiority and a belief in their mission of civilizing the "uncivilized," established a vast network of schools, churches, and administrative systems in their colonies. The spread of the English language, British laws, and institutions became tools for cultural assimilation and exerting control over colonial populations. However, this also fostered the emergence of new cultural hybridities that not only influenced the colonies but also shaped British culture itself.

It is important to acknowledge the coercive and sometimes violent methods employed during the expansion of the British Empire. The empire's history is not without instances of exploitation, oppression, and resistance. The British often employed military force to subjugate local populations, leading to conflicts and uprisings such as the Indian Rebellion of 1857 or the Mau Mau uprising in Kenya. These events highlight the complex and often turbulent nature of imperial expansion, shedding light on the tensions between imperial ambitions and the desire for self-determination among colonial subjects.

Furthermore, the expansion of the British Empire had far-reaching repercussions on both the colonizers and the colonized. On one hand, Britain's imperial ventures fueled its economic growth, technological advancements, and global influence. On the other hand, the colonies experienced both positive and negative outcomes. The imposition of British rule disrupted local economies, traditional cultures, and political structures. However, the empire also brought infrastructural development, education, healthcare, and legal systems, leaving a complex legacy that varies from one colony to another. Understanding the economic, political, cultural, and military forces at play allows us to appreciate the complexities and impact of this global empire. While acknowledging the darker aspects of imperialism, we must also recognize the influence of the British Empire in shaping our modern world. By exploring this topic in a professional, academic, and approachable manner, this book aims to shed light on the expansion of the British Empire and its lasting legacies.

Chapter 7: The Windsors and the World Wars

George V and World War I

Born on June 3, 1865, George V, originally known as Prince George Frederick Ernest Albert, was the second son of Edward VII and Queen Alexandra. Following the untimely death of his elder brother, George ascended to the throne in 1910, assuming the title of king. Unbeknownst to him at the time, his reign would be fraught with the challenges of World War I, a conflict that would shape not only his reign but the fate of nations across the globe.

As the Great War unfolded and Europe was embroiled in a devastating conflict, George V found himself at the helm of a nation divided by its decision to enter the war. Great Britain, traditionally known for its imperial endeavors, faced a crucial choice that would have far-reaching consequences. And it was within this context that George V assumed a pivotal role as the symbolic leader of the British people.

Throughout the war, George V diligently performed his duty as a figurehead, seeking to rally the nation's morale in times of turmoil. In an era before the advent of television and social media, the British public relied heavily on the monarchy for reassurance and guidance. George V recognized this responsibility and made it a priority to visit wounded soldiers and provide them with emotional support during hospital visits. These interactions with the brave soldiers who sacrificed so much undoubtedly left an indelible mark on the king, deepening his understanding of the horrors of war and amplifying his commitment to ending the conflict swiftly and justly.

Despite being a constitutional monarch with limited political power, George V was not a passive bystander during the war. On the contrary, he actively engaged with his government, often meeting with Prime Minister David Lloyd George to discuss war strategies and the unfolding events. Such engagements allowed him to voice his opinions and offer guidance, serving as an influential force behind the scenes.

One of George V's notable contributions to the war effort was his decision to change the royal family's Germanic name from the House of Saxe-Coburg and Gotha to the House of Windsor in July 1917. This move was motivated by a desire to distance the monarchy from its German origins at a time when anti-German sentiment was rampant in Britain due to the war. The name change not only symbolized the king's commitment to his adopted country but also helped to quell public discontent and reinforce national unity.

However, it is important to note that George V's role during World War I extended beyond symbolism and name changes. As the conflict raged on, he became increasingly influential in diplomatic affairs. For instance, in 1918, the king lent his support to Prime Minister Lloyd George's proposal to hold peace negotiations with the Central Powers. This support further bolstered the government's position and provided a sense of legitimacy to the negotiations, ultimately contributing to the Treaty of Versailles and the end of the war.

While George V undeniably made important contributions to the war effort, it is essential to acknowledge that his reign was not without controversy. The decision to continue certain traditional activities, such as hunting and horse racing, during the war drew criticism from some who believed that such leisure pursuits were incompatible with the gravity of the conflict. However, it is worth understanding that the king's participation in these activities was driven by a desire to maintain a sense of stability and normalcy amidst the chaos of war, rather than a lack of empathy for the plight of his people. While faced with immense challenges, he rose to the occasion, diligently supporting the war effort and providing solace to those affected by the conflict. His decision to change the royal family name and his involvement in diplomatic affairs showcased his willingness to adapt and navigate the complexities of the time. Ultimately, George V proved to be a monarch who steadfastly upheld his duty to his people, leaving a lasting legacy in the annals of history.

Abdication crisis of Edward VIII

To begin, it is essential to understand the circumstances that led to the Abdication crisis. Edward VIII, known as the Prince of Wales before his accession to the throne, had long been perceived as a somewhat wayward and unconventional royal. His fondness for socializing with the fashionable set, including divorced and married women, had already garnered attention and criticism. However, it was his desire to marry Wallis Simpson, an American woman who had divorced her first husband and was in the process of divorcing her second, that sent shockwaves throughout the monarchy and the government.

The British public's reaction to news of the proposed marriage was mixed. Many were sympathetic to the king's desire to marry the person he loved, regardless of her past. However, a significant portion of society was deeply conservative and held traditional values, viewing divorce as a scandalous and immoral practice. This division in public opinion set the stage for a clash between those who supported the king and those who believed that he could not, in good conscience, marry a divorced woman who was still undergoing legal proceedings.

The political establishment, represented by the Prime Minister at the time, Stanley Baldwin, found itself in a difficult position. Baldwin and his advisors were acutely aware of the potential constitutional crisis that could arise from the king's marriage. They recognized the complications that could emerge if Edward VIII's subjects were unconvinced of Wallis Simpson's suitability as a queen. Additionally, the British government was heavily influenced by the Church of England, which sharply criticized divorce. Ultimately, after exploratory discussions and careful consideration, Baldwin and his cabinet decided that the king's proposed marriage to Wallis Simpson was untenable and incompatible with his position as the head of state and the Church of England.

This decision led to a series of high-stakes negotiations between Edward VIII and the government, culminating in the king's shocking announcement to abdicate the throne on December 11, 1936. In his famous radio broadcast, Edward VIII explained his decision, emphasizing his love for Wallis Simpson and his belief that he could not fulfill his duties to the nation without her by his side. He expressed his hope that the British public would understand and support his choice.

The Abdication crisis created a deep rift within the royal family itself. King Edward VIII's abdication meant that he would be succeeded by his younger brother, Albert, who became King George VI. This unexpected turn of events thrust George VI into a role he had never anticipated, and it placed significant strain on the relationship between the two brothers. The new king faced the immense challenge of restoring stability to a monarchy that had been rocked by scandal and controversy.

Furthermore, the Abdication crisis had broader implications for the British monarchy and the nation as a whole. It laid bare the conflicts between traditional social expectations and the personal desires of the ruling monarch. The crisis also highlighted the evolving role of the media in shaping public opinion, as newspapers played a tremendous role in reporting and influencing public sentiment throughout the saga. Moreover, the Abdication crisis further eroded the idea of royal infallibility, as the scandal shattered the traditional image of the monarchy as a moral and exemplary institution.

In many ways, the Abdication crisis of Edward VIII marked a turning point in British history. The fallout from this event forced the monarchy to adapt to changing societal values and demands. It also strengthened the bonds between the monarchy, the government, and the people, as a greater sense of accountability and transparency was sought in the wake of the crisis. Ultimately, the Abdication crisis laid the groundwork for a more modern and accepting monarchy that would face numerous trials and tribulations in the years to come. It revealed the fragility and adaptability of the monarchy, as it navigated a constitutional crisis that threatened its very foundations. The crisis left an indelible mark on the royal family, reshaping its dynamics and forcing it to confront its own fallibility. Additionally, the Abdication crisis reflected wider societal changes and set the stage for a monarchy that would better align with the values and aspirations of the British people.

Chapter 8: Elizabeth II and modern monarchy

Queen Elizabeth II's reign and modernizing the monarchy

Throughout her reign, Queen Elizabeth II has consistently demonstrated a commitment to modernizing the monarchy and ensuring its relevance in contemporary society. In the early years of her reign, she recognized the need to connect with her subjects on a more personal level. She broke from tradition by inviting television cameras into her private life and allowing the public to witness royal events such as weddings and births. This newfound openness helped to humanize the monarchy and establish a closer bond between the Queen and her people.

Another hallmark of Queen Elizabeth II's reign has been the focus on inclusivity and diversity. The Queen has made a concerted effort to embrace the multicultural and multi-faith nature of modern Britain. She has ensured that various religious ceremonies are represented in the royal calendar and has actively sought to include individuals from diverse backgrounds in her official engagements. This signal of inclusivity has played a crucial role in maintaining the monarchy's relevance and appeal to a broad range of people across the United Kingdom and the Commonwealth.

Queen Elizabeth II has also been at the forefront of technological advancements during her reign. She recognized the importance of harnessing the power of technology to connect with people in new and innovative ways. The Queen became the first British monarch to send an email in 1976 and has since embraced social media platforms such as Twitter and Instagram to engage with the public directly. By utilizing these platforms, she has demonstrated an adaptability to the changing media landscape and has been successful in reaching a wider audience, particularly among the younger generation.

In addition to embracing new technologies, Queen Elizabeth II has been an advocate for environmental sustainability and conservation. She has emphasized the importance of protecting the natural world and has taken several steps to reduce the environmental impact of the royal household. From implementing energy-saving measures in royal residences to promoting sustainable initiatives, the Queen has been a champion for environmentally conscious practices. These efforts have not only helped modernize the monarchy but also position it as an influential force in promoting sustainability and combating climate change.

Furthermore, Queen Elizabeth II has played a pivotal role in shaping the modern Commonwealth. She has recognized the need for the Commonwealth to evolve and reflect the changing dynamics of the global stage. Under her leadership, the Commonwealth has become a platform for addressing key global issues such as poverty alleviation, gender equality, and youth empowerment. The Queen's commitment to the Commonwealth has helped modernize its role from a largely ceremonial and symbolic institution to a dynamic and impactful organization that fosters collaboration among its member nations.

It is worth noting that Queen Elizabeth II's efforts to modernize the monarchy have not diminished the deep-rooted traditions and ceremonial aspects associated with it. Despite embracing change, the Queen has always prioritized preserving the rich history and heritage of the British monarchy. She has continued to carry out numerous ceremonial duties and rituals that have been handed down through generations, such as the State Opening of Parliament and the Trooping the Colour. These traditions serve as a reminder of the monarchy's enduring presence and reinforce its role as a symbol of national unity and continuity. Her initiatives to connect with the public, embrace inclusivity, adapt to technological advancements, promote environmental sustainability, and empower the Commonwealth have all played a significant role in ensuring the monarchy's relevance in the modern world. Through her leadership, Queen Elizabeth II has successfully navigated the challenges of a rapidly changing society while retaining the monarchy's place as a beloved and respected institution.

Royal weddings and controversies

One of the key controversies surrounding royal weddings involves the question of whether they are mere spectacles or political maneuvers. Critics argue that these lavish events serve a strategic purpose, aiming to consolidate power or foster diplomatic alliances. Indeed, throughout history, royal weddings have been used as a means to strengthen political ties, forge peace agreements, or solidify the legitimacy of a monarch's rule. Yet, it is important to view these weddings as more than just political tools. They are also celebrations of love, family, and cultural heritage, where individuals from different backgrounds come together to honor their shared traditions. By acknowledging this duality, we can appreciate royal weddings as both significant political undertakings and joyous occasions that unite people.

Another controversy associated with royal weddings revolves around the financial implications. Critics argue that these extravagant celebrations place a heavy burden on taxpayers, who bear the cost of security, arrangements, and even the venues themselves. Opponents often question the justifiability of allocating considerable funds for such events, especially in times of economic hardship. It is crucial to address these concerns and examine the economic impact of royal weddings in a broader context. While it is true that these celebrations can incur substantial costs, they also generate significant revenue through tourism, media coverage, and cultural promotion. The spectacle of a royal wedding attracts global attention, enticing visitors to explore the host country and boosting local businesses. Thus, it can be argued that royal weddings, despite their expense, have the potential to provide long-term economic benefits, creating a favorable trade-off for the host nation.

Controversies surrounding royal weddings are not solely limited to political and economic dimensions; they can also arise from societal expectations and public scrutiny. Traditional gender roles and patriarchal norms often take center stage during these highly publicized events, sparking debates about gender equality and modern values. The scrutiny faced by royal brides, in particular, is notable. They are expected to adhere to strict standards of beauty, etiquette, and behavior, often subjected to intense media scrutiny and public commentary. Debates about body image, submit to traditional norms, and conform to societal expectations. Critiques of these gendered expectations are necessary to encourage a broader dialogue about representation in public life and promote a more inclusive and progressive society.

Moreover, controversies surrounding royal weddings are frequently intertwined with questions of identity, race, and class. The British royal family, for instance, has faced criticism for their historically exclusive practices and lack of diversity. As the institution becomes more reflective of contemporary society, these issues are brought into sharp focus. The marriage of Prince Harry, a member of the British royal family, to Meghan Markle, an African American actress, was met with both excitement and controversy. It brought to the forefront discussions about racial dynamics, multiculturalism, and the role of monarchy in a diverse society. This significant event underscored the need for institutions to adapt and embrace inclusivity, while also highlighting the challenges and opportunities that arise from such transformations. The political undertones, financial implications, societal expectations, and questions of identity surrounding these events have fueled public fascination and debate throughout history. By acknowledging and addressing these controversies, we can engage in meaningful discussions about the role of monarchy, cultural heritage, and societal values. Ultimately, royal weddings can serve as catalysts for change, prompting us to reflect on our traditions, challenge norms, and work towards a more inclusive and equitable future.

Chapter 9: The future of the British monarchy

Succession and the role of the monarchy in modern society

As the world rapidly evolves, the position and significance of monarchies within modern society is a subject of great interest and debate. In this discussion, we will explore the concept of succession and how the role of monarchy has adapted to the changing times. By shedding light on their contemporary functions, we hope to provide a comprehensive understanding of the significance and relevance of monarchies in the present era.

Historical Context of Monarchy:

To truly appreciate the place of monarchy in modern society, it is essential to comprehend its historical context. Monarchies have deep roots tracing back to ancient civilizations, where kings and queens ruled with divine authority, entrusted with maintaining order and prosperity within their realms. This system of governance remained prominent in various forms throughout the Middle Ages and the Renaissance period, with rulers often claiming a divine right to rule.

However, as societies progressed and embraced democratic

principles, monarchies sought to adapt and redefine their roles. Over time, constitutional monarchies emerged, with monarchs assuming ceremonial and symbolic duties while the actual governing responsibilities shifted to elected bodies. This transition marks a crucial turning point in the role of monarchy, leading us to examine its current significance.

Contemporary Functions of Monarchy:

In the modern era, the role of monarchy varies greatly across countries and cultures, often characterized by a delicate balance of tradition, symbolism, and public service. One notable function of constitutional monarchies is their ability to represent the unity and history of a nation. Monarchs act as figureheads, embodying the values and identity of their respective countries, providing a sense of continuity and stability in times of rapid change.

Another critical function of monarchy lies in promoting diplomacy and international relations. Monarchs often serve as ambassadors, fostering goodwill and creating connections with other nations. By undertaking official visits and hosting state visits, they can contribute to building strong relationships between countries, facilitating cultural exchanges, and supporting global cooperation.

Furthermore, many monarchies have developed a philanthropic role, engaging in charitable endeavors and championing noble causes. By lending their patronage to various organizations, monarchs can raise awareness, mobilize resources, and ultimately have a positive impact on society. Their involvement in humanitarian work reinforces their relevance in addressing pressing issues faced by their nations.

Critique and Defense of Monarchy:

While the role of monarchy in modern society is widely acknowledged and respected, it is not immune to criticism. Critics argue that monarchies are an outdated institution, incompatible with the principles of democracy and equality. They claim that hereditary succession undermines the democratic rights of citizens, depriving them of the ability to elect their head of state. Additionally, resources allocated to the maintenance of a royal family could be used for social welfare programs.

On the other hand, supporters of monarchy contend that the institution provides a sense of identity, tradition, and stability. They emphasize the moderating effect of constitutional monarchies, serving as a check on government power and ensuring the continuity of the state across successive administrations. Monarchs, being apolitical figures, can unite their nations without the divisiveness often associated with partisan politics. Monarchies, through their symbolic, diplomatic, and philanthropic functions, contribute to the cultural and social fabric of their nations. While it is true that monarchies face criticism for their perceived undemocratic nature, they also offer a balance of power, stability, and continuity that can complement democratic systems. Ultimately, the significance of monarchies in contemporary society lies in striking a delicate balance between a nation's heritage and the demands of the present.

Public perception and challenges facing the monarchy

One of the primary factors influencing public perception of the monarchy is its historical role and traditions. Monarchies have often been associated with tradition, continuity, and stability. However, as societies have become more diverse and multicultural, these traditional values can be seen as restrictive or exclusive. This poses a challenge for monarchies, as they must strive to balance their historical legacy while adapting to the changing demands and expectations of a diverse public. To maintain positive public perception, it is crucial for monarchies to actively engage with their constituents, listen to their concerns, and promote inclusivity and diversity in their actions and policies.

Contemporary challenges facing monarchical systems are shaped by the ongoing democratization of society, the rise of social media, and increased scrutiny of public figures. Monarchs must navigate the delicate line between maintaining their symbolic roles and actively participating in public affairs. The challenge lies in striking the right balance, as being too distant from public concerns can lead to perceptions of elitism and irrelevance, whilst being too involved in political matters may erode the neutrality and impartiality that monarchies should uphold. Transparency, accessibility, and responsiveness are crucial for modern monarchies to address these challenges, as they foster trust and enable the public to feel connected and valued.

Another challenge facing monarchical systems is the potential for controversies and scandals to undermine public perception.

As symbols of national identity, monarchs represent the values and ideals of their respective nations. Any personal or institutional wrongdoing by members of the monarchy can have a significant impact on public perception. Monarchs must adhere to strict moral and ethical standards and be held accountable for their actions. Institutions supporting the monarchy should also have robust mechanisms in place to address misconduct or irregularities promptly. Public perception can be positively influenced when the monarchy demonstrates a commitment to justice, fairness, and accountability.

Legitimacy is another critical element influencing public perception. Monarchies must continually justify their existence and demonstrate their relevance in a rapidly changing world. The focus should not solely be on historical continuity but also on the genuine contributions and tangible benefits that monarchies bring to society. This means actively engaging in philanthropy, promoting cultural heritage, and leading initiatives that address societal challenges. By demonstrating their commitment to the welfare and development of their nations, monarchies can enhance their legitimacy and garner public support.

Education and public outreach are essential tools for monarchies to shape and improve public perception. Promoting awareness and understanding of the role and functions of the monarchy can dispel misconceptions and foster appreciation for its contributions. Monarchies can utilize modern communication channels, including social media, to engage with a wider audience and share their activities, initiatives, and milestones. Embracing transparency and openness enables the public to feel connected and involved, strengthening the bond between the monarchy and its citizens. Monarchies face challenges in adapting to societal changes, addressing controversies, maintaining legitimacy, and fostering inclusivity. By embracing transparency, accountability, accessibility, and public outreach, monarchies can overcome these challenges and enhance public perception and support. It is through proactive engagement, continuous adaptation, and a commitment to the welfare of their nations that monarchies can build positive and enduring public perception for generations to come.

Chapter 10: Conclusion

Recap of key monarchs and their impact on British history

One of the earliest monarchs worth mentioning is Alfred the Great (849-899), who ruled the Anglo-Saxon kingdom of Wessex. Alfred is revered as a wise and visionary leader who successfully defended his kingdom against Viking invasions. His reign marked a period of innovation and cultural renewal, as he promoted literacy and learning throughout his kingdom. Alfred's efforts to establish a legal code, the Domboc, and his dedication to education laid the foundation for a future unified England.

Jumping forward several centuries, we encounter William the Conqueror (1028-1087), who is best known for his victory at the Battle of Hastings in 1066. By defeating King Harold II of England, William established Norman rule over the country and initiated a period of intense political and social change. His reign led to the merging of Norman and Anglo-Saxon cultures, resulting in a new ruling elite and a linguistic shift toward the French language. The Norman Conquest also brought about significant changes in the feudal system, with the introduction of the Domesday Book, a comprehensive survey of landownership and taxation.

The Tudor dynasty, which reigned from 1485 to 1603, left an indelible mark on British history. Beginning with Henry VII, the

Tudor monarchs played a vital role in transforming England into a centralized and powerful nation-state. Henry VII's reign saw the end of the Wars of the Roses and the establishment of the Tudor dynasty. His son, Henry VIII, is perhaps the most well-known Tudor monarch, largely due to his six marriages and the English Reformation. Henry's break with the Catholic Church and the establishment of the Church of England had profound implications for religious, political, and social life in England.

Elizabeth I (1558-1603), the daughter of Henry VIII and Anne Boleyn, is often regarded as one of the most influential monarchs in British history. Her long reign came to symbolize the Golden Age, characterized by economic expansion, naval exploration, and cultural flourishing. Elizabeth's leadership during the Spanish Armada crisis of 1588 marked a pivotal moment in English history, as her successful defense against Spanish invasion solidified England's status as a global power. Furthermore, Elizabeth's patronage of the arts and literature gave rise to a flourishing of creativity, with luminaries such as William Shakespeare and Francis Drake thriving under her rule.

Moving into the 17th century, the English Civil War and the subsequent Interregnum brought about a seismic shift in British political and social structures. During this tumultuous period, King Charles I clashed with Parliament over issues of royal authority, leading to a bloody conflict that resulted in his execution in 1649. This marked the first time in English history that a monarch had been put to death by his own subjects. The Interregnum, under Oliver Cromwell's rule, initiated a short-lived republic known as the Commonwealth of England. Cromwell's leadership, though authoritarian, saw the emergence of England as a major power in Europe, particularly through naval triumphs against the Dutch and Spanish.

The Glorious Revolution of 1688 ushered in a new era in British history, as William of Orange and his wife, Mary II, ascended to the throne jointly. The revolution established the principle of constitutional monarchy, with the monarch bound by laws and sharing power with Parliament. Furthermore, the Bill of Rights, passed in 1689, enshrined individual liberties and limited the authority of the crown. The Glorious Revolution solidified the Protestant supremacy in England and marked a significant step towards the establishment of a modern liberal democratic state.

The Victorian era, spanning from 1837 to 1901, witnessed the reign of Queen Victoria, a monarch whose influence extended far beyond her own era. Victoria's reign saw the height of British industrialization, the expansion of the British Empire, and significant socio-cultural transformations. The Victorian period was marked by advancements in technology, such as the development of railways, which revolutionized transportation. Victoria's reign also saw the rise of social movements, including women's suffrage and the abolition of slavery, reflecting a society grappling with pressing issues of social justice. From Alfred the Great forging the foundations of a unified England to Queen Victoria presiding over a period of immense change, each monarch has contributed to the intricate tapestry of British history. Whether through military triumphs, political reform, or cultural patronage, these monarchs have left a legacy that continues to shape the United Kingdom. Understanding their reigns and their impact is essential for comprehending the rich and complex history of Britain.

Reflection on the enduring relevance of the British monarchy.

With its rich history, elaborate ceremonies, and iconic figures, it continues to captivate the public's imagination. Even in a world of rapidly changing political systems and evolving societal structures, the British monarchy remains an influential and central institution. This reflection aims to explore the enduring relevance of the British monarchy, examining its ties to national identity, the constitutional role it plays, and the cultural significance it holds for the United Kingdom and beyond.

National Identity:
The British monarchy has long been intertwined with the national identity of the United Kingdom. It symbolizes the country's heritage and acts as a unifying force, transcending social, cultural, and regional divisions. The monarchy provides a tangible link to the past, connecting the present generation with the shared experiences and achievements of their ancestors. The regal figureheads, such as Queen Elizabeth II, embody the values and traditions that define the nation, reinforcing a sense of national pride and cohesion.

Constitutional Role:
While the British monarchy holds a predominantly symbolic position, it plays a vital constitutional role in the governance of the United Kingdom. The monarchy, as a non-partisan entity, provides a neutral and stabilizing influence within the country's political system. It acts as a constitutional safeguard, where the monarch's role includes granting royal assent to legislation, appointing prime ministers, and participating in the ceremonial opening of parliamentary sessions. This impartiality ensures that political power does not rest solely in the hands of elected officials, maintaining a balance between tradition and modern

governance.

Cultural Significance:
Beyond its constitutional role, the British monarchy holds immense cultural significance, both domestically and internationally. The ceremonial traditions of the monarchy, such as the Changing of the Guard at Buckingham Palace or the Trooping the Colour, are globally recognized manifestations of British heritage. These cultural rituals, steeped in history, attract millions of tourists each year, contributing to the country's economy and promoting an understanding of British traditions and values.

The monarchy's patronage of various charitable organizations also plays a crucial role in the social fabric of the United Kingdom. Royal involvement in philanthropic pursuits helps to raise awareness and funds for countless causes, ranging from mental health initiatives to wildlife conservation. Through their patronages and personal involvement, members of the royal family contribute to the betterment of society, inspiring others to engage in acts of service and compassion.

Public Engagement and Tourism:
Apart from its cultural role, the British monarchy's enduring relevance is also reflected in the public's avid engagement. The royal family is a subject of immense interest and scrutiny, with their lives and actions regularly making headlines around the world. Therefore, the British monarchy has a unique ability to generate excitement, captivate the public's imagination, and establish a sense of continuity across generations.

The monarchy's popularity is notably demonstrated by the

extensive tourism revenue it brings into the United Kingdom. The allure of visiting iconic royal residences, such as Buckingham Palace or Windsor Castle, draws visitors from all corners of the globe. These establishments act as living museums, allowing tourists to experience the grandeur and history associated with the British monarchy.

Adaptability and Modernization:
Another key aspect of the monarchy's enduring relevance lies in its adaptability and ability to embrace modernization. While rooted in tradition, the monarchy has proven its capacity to evolve with the times, ensuring its continued relevance in contemporary society. Queen Elizabeth II, for example, has successfully navigated countless changes in societal norms during her reign, adapting the monarchy's public image to align with modern values.

Furthermore, the royal family's use of social media platforms has allowed them to connect directly with the public in unprecedented ways. By leveraging digital platforms, they can foster greater transparency and engagement, breaking down barriers and demystifying the monarchy in the eyes of the public. As a cornerstone of British heritage, the monarchy serves as a unifying force and a symbol of stability. By embracing tradition whilst simultaneously adapting to the modern world, the British monarchy continues to captivate the imagination of the public and maintain its relevance in the 21st century.

Printed in Great Britain
by Amazon